More animals were involved in the First World War than in any previous conflict. This book explores the role of some of the creatures taking part and the contribution they, and British animal welfare organisations, made. The horse, camel and dog feature here, but so too do the pigeon, glow worm and slug. How certain animals in Britain itself were affected by the war is also considered: dogs and their owners, for example, or the response of London Zoo. Finally, it explores what happened to the dogs and horses who survived the war, and how those animals who did not were remembered.

One of the most famous recruiting posters of them all: Forward to Victory.

Forward to Victory
ENLIST NOW

BRITAIN IN 1914:
A HORSE-DRAWN SOCIETY

Images can mislead. Early 20th-century society – including the nature of the war which broke out in 1914 – is often viewed as modern. Motor cars, electric trams and petrol-driven buses were indeed familiar sights to many in Britain's towns and cities at that time. Similarly, tanks, motor vehicles and aeroplanes were used in the First World War. But when war broke out Britain was still very much a horse-drawn society and as a result more animals were to be involved in this conflict than in any that had preceded it.

Drawing on a (incomplete) 1909 police census of horses, it is thought that there were probably three million working horses in Britain in 1914 – only 500,000 below the 1902 peak. Whilst the largest concentration of horses was in the countryside, they still played their part in transporting both people and goods within and (although

Piccadilly Circus at the turn of the 20th century, showing hansom cabs, horse-drawn buses and single horses with riders.

less significantly) between places. Horse buses, horse trams, hansom cabs and private carriages were still in regular use in 1914. It was more usual, however, to hire rather than own horses in London. Companies offered horses for hire for both commercial or public use and for private use. Similarly, horse-drawn vehicles delivered most goods. Horses too were essential for shunting in railway goods yards and station sidings, and in the mills, factories and collieries. Additionally, around 200,000 horses were kept exclusively for hunting.

The presence and needs of such a high horse population impacted on both urban and rural society. Britain could supply the number of horses required annually but feeding them was a challenge. As a result, about 15 million acres worldwide were devoted to producing fodder for the nation's horses. Corn and oats for horses were both grown in Britain and supplemented with imports.

Horses pulling railway carriages in France. This was a common sight in pre-war Britain too.

The Army too relied on the horse. Feeding horses transported overseas would therefore also require considerable resources. The Army had just 80 motor vehicles in August 1914, compared to over 20,000 horses. By November 1918, however, millions of horses, mules and other animals from Britain and around the world had become involved in the conflict. When it ended, about half the Army's horses were serving on the Western Front; others were elsewhere in Europe and the Middle East. The Army Veterinary Corps met the needs of (primarily) sick and injured horses. It too had expanded – from 364 officers and 934 other ranks in 1914 to 1,306 officers and 41,755 men of other ranks by the end of the war.

Horse-drawn buses outside the Bank of England in the years just before the First World War.

3

THE SUPPLY AND MOBILISATION OF HORSES

The Army had long recognised that it would require – and speedily – tens of thousands more horses on the outbreak of a major war. A voluntary Horse Registration Scheme was established in 1887 to identify those owners willing to sell (together with the agreed sale price for) their mounts. In return, the Army paid them a 10-shilling annual retainer fee for each horse listed. In 1888 the government acquired powers to requisition all horses in the event of a national emergency, and in 1909 the police undertook a horse census (mentioned earlier).

In its plans for war, the Army would immediately increase the number of its horses through both the Registration Scheme (10,000) and impressment (130,000), thereby making an initial total of over 160,000 animals. The plans succeeded: by mid-August 1914, the Army had seven times its peacetime number of horses – but not without some anxiety. Three children (Poppy, Lionel and Freda Hewlett) wrote from Lancashire to ask Lord Kitchener, the Secretary of State for War, to exempt their pony from enlistment. He replied immediately, stating that no horse under 15 hands belonging to them would be requisitioned. There was a public assembly of commandeered horses in almost every community – they were even tethered in the Tower of London moat.

Overall, between August 1914 and June 1918 some 450,000 horses were supplied from within the UK for military purposes. But the War Office had also planned to buy horses from overseas. Tens of thousands of foreign horses were purchased either by Britain

Lord Kitchener received a personal petition from three children about their pet pony.

4

or by other territories in the British Empire. They were sourced both from within the Empire – Australia, Canada, India, New Zealand and South Africa – and beyond, notably Spain, Portugal, China and South America. Similarly, and for the first time, Britain had decided to supplement pack and draught horses with tens of thousands of mules. Previously, in 1913, the Army had bought just three.

Securing and transporting both horses and mules was reasonably well planned. Britain sent purchasing commissions to Portugal, Spain, North and South America and Australasia. Some two-thirds of Britain's horses

Capturing old and new worlds: streams of lorries pass columns of horses on a French road.

AT THE FRONT!

Every fit Briton should join our brave men at the Front.

ENLIST NOW.

(and most mules) from overseas were imported from North and South America; 40,000 mules arrived from the USA alone. New depots to recuperate and train horses and mules from North America were established near Ormskirk, Lancashire, for those landing at Liverpool, and at nearby Shirehampton for those disembarking at Bristol.

More early propaganda put out by the British government emphasising the role of horses at the Front.

MAKING HORSES READY FOR WAR

The Army required different types of horses to fulfil a range of duties. Factors taken into account included their breed, size and strength. Horses were mostly assigned to the cavalry, artillery (differentiated between 'light' and 'heavy') or transport, together with mules, as draught animals.

The cavalry regiments which formed part of the British Expeditionary Force (BEF) were accompanied by their trained and well-disciplined horses. Other horses and mules, purchased following the outbreak of the war, might be assigned to the BEF or made ready in Britain itself for the war. With an expanded Army came the need for more (new) horses – especially, as noted, from overseas. The Army Remount Services/Department, which had also overseen the original acquisition of the horses, now came into its own.

British cavalry pictured at the Western Front, here using their saddles as armchairs.

A 'remount' can be defined as a horse designated for military service but yet to be assigned for duty. Such horses were sent to special (normally Army-owned) centres known as 'depots'. At the start of the First World War there were depots in Dublin, Woolwich, Melton Mowbray, Arborfield (near Wokingham in Berkshire) and Chiddingfold (near Godalming). Together they were responsible for training 1,200 animals at a time. In addition to Ormskirk and Shirehampton, major new depots were established at Romsey (to house horses and mules from the USA) and Swaythling, both near the port of Southampton. Swaythling oversaw the transport of most horses and mules to France.

There were also several smaller depots. At their peak the depots held 60,000 animals.

A typical large depot might possess most or all of the following: a harness room, shoeing shed, forge, horse shelters, dip, veterinary hospital, and kraal. The horses and mules brought to the Romsey depot were led through the streets from the railway, often in a semi-wild state, and held in the kraal. The kraal had hessian to provide extra protection – a material which was usually quickly eaten by the mules. By 1916 Romsey depot had ten squadrons, each with 40 'rough riders' whose task was to break in the animals. There was medical and dental support should the men be injured in the process. Each man was responsible for three horses and fed them five times daily. On departing from the depot, each man would ride one horse and lead another to Southampton docks.

Initially, only men were involved with breaking in horses. However, when Russley Park depot, near Swindon in Wiltshire, opened in 1916 it was staffed entirely by women, most of whom were already experienced with horses.

Lieutenant Mike Rimington of Shrewsbury was one Horse Whisperer of his day, gaining 'complete ascendancy over the animals by kindness and tact'.

Gathering food for the horses at an Army remount depot.

TRANSPORTING HORSES TO AND SERVING THE WESTERN FRONT

Some 40,000 horses and mules accompanied the British Expeditionary Force; each Division of 18,000 men was assigned 5,600 horses. These and subsequent animals needed to be transported to a port (normally Southampton), hoisted individually aboard ship and stabled in her hold before undergoing the crossing. On arrival in France they would be transported by rail to the Western Front.

These unfamiliar experiences, on top of being confined in crowded conditions, were frightening for the horses. They often caught diseases or suffered (fatal) heart attacks. Up to 30 per cent of horses might die in transit between Britain and the Western Front, but the norm was less than half of this. If two per cent or less died on a journey, there was an extra payment per horse for that shipment.

These two images from the earliest stages of the war show the muster and transportation of horses to the Western Front, and the use of special winches to raise and lower the animals to and from the ship's deck.

Army expectation and experience of horses on the battlefront depended on their function. A cavalry regiment usually comprised 549 men and, excluding reserves, 528 horses, 74 draught horses and six pack horses. The importance of the cavalry, however, deemed so central at the outset, diminished as the nature of the war on the Western Front changed. The trench, rather than the cavalry charge, symbolised the conflict for most of its duration; the number of cavalry horses declined accordingly. In addition to engagements, cavalry horses carried messengers and were used for reconnaissance.

When walking, a cavalry horse was expected to cover four miles in an hour (excluding halts); when trotting this increased to eight miles; and, if galloping, reached 15 miles. Supply horses travelled up to three miles in an hour; the pack horse or mule slightly more. Two, four or six pairs of horses could pull proportionately more than their solo efforts. But appropriate pairing was essential if every grouped horse were to pull equally – be it artillery, (general) supplies or ambulances – and respond in unison to any difficulties encountered.

Whenever possible horses kept close to one side of a road, near to trees, walls or buildings. Their shadows might conceal soldiers from observation or overhead attack. When resting, horses needed to be able to turn their backs to the wind and be tethered together. This was termed a picket line; each cavalry horse carried its own picketing post. Grooms – in one instance a 12-year-old Indian boy – would be on hand. Everyone needed to be wary, however, of horse kicks, though these were more predictable than mules' kicks: horses only kick backwards, but mules can kick in any direction.

This photograph from 1916 captures one of the last uses of a military tactic that, having persisted for thousands of years, would be all but a memory by the war's end: the cavalry charge.

Horses were used for carrying extra ammunition for their rider.

HORSE WELFARE AND HOSPITALS

Some 450,000 horses served the British Army in the war. About one in seven horses died annually, mostly because of illness, hunger or the environment. Enemy action (usually bullets or shrapnel) accounted for less than a quarter of horse deaths on the Western Front. Fortunately gas was not a major problem either. Few horses received gas respirators, and those that were issued were often chewed, as horses thought that they contained fodder.

Horses, if affected by the war, were more likely to experience illness or injury than death at the Front. Consequently, food and veterinary care were vital concerns. It has been claimed that more fodder than ammunition was sent to the Western Front: 3 million tons of oats and 2.5 million tons of pressed hay. Even so, fodder was often rationed. A horse hauling supplies normally received a daily fodder allowance of 20lbs instead of the recommended 25lbs. Pulling artillery was more demanding. Such horses received 30lbs daily, taking a total of five hours to consume this amount.

Gas masks for horses, often mistaken for feed bags and chewed.

The first horses on the Western Front soon began to suffer. The initial absence of blacksmiths meant that many horses went lame because they needed to be shod. They might also be poorly, even cruelly handled or denied enough breaks for food and water. Heavy plough horses, thought to be ideal for hauling artillery but conscripted against veterinary advice, died in great numbers, partly because of frequently wet feet.

The Army Veterinary Corps oversaw the treatment of sick and wounded animals. Veterinary officers were to be found in transport, cavalry, artillery and infantry regiments and

A Blue Cross hospital in action at Serqueux in December 1914.

would treat those animals in need. There was also the Mobile Veterinary Service. This collected and evacuated the more serious cases either for treatment in the region or back in Britain. Animals would be transported by horse ambulance or rail. Those thought unlikely to recover would be shot, if death did not come naturally, which often distressed those associated with the animal. This is represented in the painting (and popular print/postcard) by Matania, *Goodbye Old Man*, showing a horse dying of his wounds as his grieving owner looks on.

Horse hospitals were both general (treating surgical and medical cases) and special (mange and skin problems). The horses, ponies and mules would be separated and sub-divided according to the treatment intended. Some 80 per cent of those animals admitted were able to return to the Front. The prefix 'Royal' was added to the Army Veterinary Corps at the war's end in recognition of its life-saving work.

Surgeons chloroforming a horse before an operation at the front.

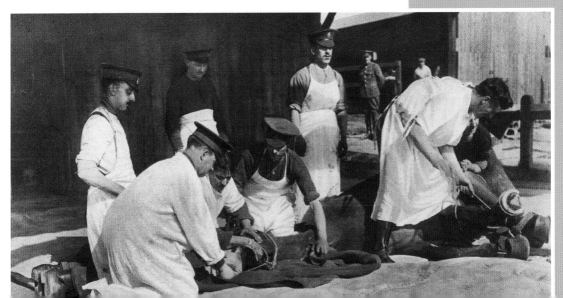

THE TRAINING AND USE OF DOGS IN WAR

Dogs have been involved in warfare since at least the medieval era. By 1914 there were war-training schools for dogs in several parts of Europe, notably Germany (some of whose dogs had been imported from Britain). But there was no such establishment in Britain itself until the first was established in 1916. This owed its existence to the persistence of Lieutenant Colonel Richardson. It was he who had supplied the one (sentry) dog in the British Army, for a Norfolk battalion which accompanied the Expeditionary Force.

Although Richardson's idea of setting up a school of instruction for military dogs was rebuffed by the War Office, he travelled to the Western Front in August 1914 with a view to training (local) ambulance dogs. Using their acute sense of smell and hearing, dogs were taught to locate immobile soldiers even if they were half-buried. The dogs went into no man's land wearing coats with the Red Cross insignia. Also strapped to their body would be a container with water or stimulant and first-aid supplies. Most active in the dark, their barking directed stretcher-bearers to their charges. Dogs might also alert bearers by retrieving something of the injured soldier's clothing.

Richardson was eventually able to convince the War Office that, with a cylinder strapped to them, dogs could be trained as messengers.
Dogs were also less

Major Richardson with some of his Red Cross dogs in the early years of the war.

MAJ. RICHARDSON & BRITISH RED CROSS DOGS

A British team emulating their Belgian Allies by using dogs to draw a machine gun in France.

susceptible to gas. A school was established at Shoeburyness in Essex. It was within earshot of the guns firing on the Western Front. The dogs thus became inured to the sound. By 1918 a bigger site was needed, and the school moved to a site near Lyndhurst in Hampshire.

Centres for abandoned dogs, notably the one at Battersea, were a major source of supply. But also families with members fighting overseas might particularly want their much-loved pets to be involved. At first dogs were trained for ambulance and messenger work. Sentry and patrol duties were added later and used in Britain as well as overseas. Recruits were assessed for each role and selected where most competent. Richardson found Lurchers (often used by poachers) the best all-rounder; Airedales and sheepdogs were best suited as messengers and sentries, and Great Danes suited as watchdogs. Training lasted for about six weeks. It included learning to wade through water and surmount barbed-wire fences. Dogs in these various capacities saved many lives.

A despatch dog in the trenches. The men were under orders never to pet or call these dogs as they went about their duties.

WAR IN THE AIR: PIGEONS AND CANARIES

Pigeons have long been used in war. During the Crusades Muslims used them to carry messages; the Christian commanders responded with falcons to intercept and kill them. The Naval Pigeon Service was the first to use them when war broke out. Released from mine sweepers, messenger or homing pigeons kept the Admiralty informed of new-laid mines. Submarines and sea-planes in distress could also release pigeons. The service saved thousands of lives in this way.

Depending on weather conditions, homing pigeons can cover 300 miles, travelling up to 75mph. The Military Pigeon Service was under the control of Lieutenant-Colonel Osman and the first pigeons were sent to the Western Front in March 1916. Initially the lofts there were adapted omnibuses, and cyclists transported pigeons to the Front in wicker crates. Later on, pigeons were released from airplanes, small balloons or tanks – although the resultant petrol fumes might disorientate them. Some 100,000 pigeons were involved in the war, mostly on the Western Front but elsewhere too, notably at Salonika.

This photograph from 1916 shows His Majesty's Pigeon Service in the act of releasing a bird from a British trench.

British motor-lorry pigeon 'lofts', transported crates of birds to the trenches; the birds were trained to return to the lofts once they'd delivered their messages.

The birds were most useful locally when telegraph or telephone links were down. Messages were written and folded into small aluminium cylinders which were clipped to the birds' legs. Birds would often be starved before release to make them more eager to return to their lofts to feed. If German pigeons were captured they might also be released with dud messages. A bell would alert an attendant to a pigeon's arrival.

In March 1918, during a nationwide campaign for the purchase of War Bonds, pigeons carried messages from some investors' homes to the Tank Bank in Trafalgar Square with the amount they wished to invest.

These young birds are being transported to a trench in the final stage of their training.

Canaries are 15 times more sensitive to the presence of gas than humans, hence their long use in coal mines. On the Western Front gas was first used in 1915, and canaries were assigned to trenches to alert the troops accordingly. Consequently, as potential life-savers, they were well cared for and frequently adopted as pets. This was less often the case with slugs, who also reacted quickly to gas.

Few had expected to see any bird life on the Western Front beyond the vulture, raven and hooded crow. Perhaps because birds understood gunfire as a form of thunder, several bird

species re-appeared fearlessly in the spring of 1915. Bombardment created shell-holes but the release of potash (a fertiliser) resulted in plant growth too. Birds used them to build nests and feed. Soldiers might protect nests, and listen to birdsong, including, it was said, that of a cuckoo during the Battle of the Somme.

A bird perching on a German shell; this photograph was taken on the Western Front in 1915. Birdsong in the trenches has become one of the enduring memories of the conflict.

'THEY ALSO SERVED': CAMELS AND OTHER LIVING CREATURES

During the First World War, for a variety of reasons, the British military and intelligence drew on more living species than in previous conflicts.

Specially adapted camel transports for the wounded on the Middle Eastern Front.

The Army's 50,000 transport camels were crucial in the campaign against the Ottoman Empire in the Middle East. There were also camel regiments, notably the Imperial Camel Corps. Carrying a rider, food, a water tank ('fantass') plus military supplies strapped to each side, they could cover between 30 and 70 miles a day. But care was necessary to meet their needs. Camels might drink between 15–25 gallons of water at one time, so troughs were required as standing in lakes or rivers would damage their feet. But given their herd instinct, camels tended to move together. So it was important to ensure that each camel had consumed enough water on each visit before the herd departed. Eating was likewise affected – camels had to avoid swallowing sand as this could cause colic, leading to fatal stomach ulcers. Like horses, they were vulnerable to mange. Arabian camels suffer with the cold: night-time exposure caused the loss of most of the 3,000 camels in the British advance on Jerusalem in late 1917.

As a consequence of the German use of gas in early 1915, the Royal Engineers' Experimental Station was established in 1916 at Porton Down near Salisbury, Wiltshire. The Royal Engineers were the most involved in British chemical warfare at this time. Animals underwent tests to assess the impact of gas and how it might best be resisted. The first main experiments involved the release of hydrogen sulphide over 100 yards upwind of a system of trenches into which caged rats were placed. Cats were also used in experiments, as were goats (their respiration is similar to humans) and monkeys. In November 1918 the monkeys were either released into the countryside or given to zoos.

A camel taking a friendly nibble on the arm of a member of the Camel Transport Corps in Palestine, 1917.

Elsewhere, goldfish were placed in water within which anti-gas masks had been soaked. Such action made it possible to identify the gas released in an attack. Less successful were attempts to use certain sea-lions – former music-hall performers under 'Captain' Woodward – to detect the presence of German submarines, despite apparently successful trials in swimming baths and a lake in North Wales. Similarly, there were futile efforts to persuade seagulls to settle on enemy periscopes. But two insects were useful: glow worms, kept in a jar to use as a safe light in the trenches, and maggots which were used as an early antibiotic.

Another type of animal altogether: camel teams were the norm in the Middle East, but ox teams prevailed in Serbia.

PETS AND THE WAR

As noted, pigeons, dogs and cats were all featured in the First World War. Cats were present in the trenches as well as aboard ships where they killed rats and other vermin, and might help to detect gas. On the Home Front they were a source of comfort to many. This was also true for dogs, and the thousands of people who kept pigeons. But, unlike for cats, public opinion was divided over dogs, and pigeons now needed to be licensed.

A drawing from the Illustrated London News showing a ratting terrier in action.

The prospect of enemy aliens communicating with their homeland by pigeon gave cause for many to shoot these birds. Early in the war the National Homing Union reminded the general public that shooting carrier pigeons was illegal. The Natural History Museum had prominent displays to help the public distinguish between carrier pigeons, woodpigeons and doves. The official advice was 'if unsure, don't shoot' and injured or dead pigeons were to be handed in to the authorities. The railways stopped transporting pigeons for home release.

It soon became illegal to keep pigeons without a licence, whatever the reason. No enemy aliens were issued with licences and, if found with pigeons (even if only for eating), they were often imprisoned. The press urged pigeon fanciers to donate their birds to the national cause: the 20,000 members of the Homing Pigeon Society in Birmingham offered 30,000 pigeons.

Keeping dogs as pets was controversial during the war. Although some dogs raised money for war charities and were deemed to be good for civilian morale, many people saw them as an unnecessary drain on resources – especially the cost and provision of food. It was argued that food for a pet dog might instead have fed a human, and calculations were made as to the shipping space used for food which went only to sustain Britain's pets. Some argued that owners should be legally limited to one dog. There were campaigns too against dog shows and the waste of effort these involved. But few shows were cancelled, and Crufts was held every year except 1918. Rosettes, however, were now awarded; cash for prizes and profits were sent to support war charities.

Although less evident than popularly believed, there was some hostility to dachshunds. Being of German origin, they were viewed as the enemy and might be attacked. In 1916, opposition to a London and North Western Railway engine called 'Dachshund' persuaded the company to rename it 'Bulldog'.

'Almost mad with joy': a contemporary sketch of the reaction of many pets to a visit by their beloved owner, freshly home from the Front.

RECENT PORTRAIT
THE OTHER CHAP.

The patriotic bulldog, whose popularity as a pet soared with the British during the conflict.

LONDON ZOO AND THE WAR

London Zoo was much affected by the war. About one-third of its 150 staff left either to enlist or to become more directly involved in the war effort. Similarly, whereas the zoo had almost 4,000 vertebrate animals in August 1914, by December 1918 this number had fallen by almost half. Visitor numbers initially, however, were among the best since it had first opened in 1828. Fewer visitors in 1917 and 1918 was attributed to the government ban on most (cheaper) railway excursion fares in order to discourage leisure travel. Income from ticket sales suffered throughout, as admission was either free or reduced for those in the forces and their families, as well as refugees from Continental Europe.

This elephant in Sheffield was carrying out important war work, hauling 'eight tons easily' in every load.

London Zoo had fewer animals as the war progressed. Partly to reduce the food bill, those animals which died were not normally replaced. Similarly, for various reasons, the zoo killed those which could be used as food and easily replaced once peace had returned – as indeed happened. In February 1918, for instance, just before food rationing began in London, the zoo killed its bison, distributing cuts among the staff. Overall food shortages meant visitors also became less willing to give titbits to animals, such as buns to the elephants. In fact, this practice was eventually banned altogether. The zoo increased the animals' allocation, but the bun-loving elephants still searched through people's bags. The zoo itself also generated more food, which benefitted both the animals and also patients at local hospitals, where cuts of meat were donated.

The zoo served the wider public through its exhibitions. These included information on how to deal with houseflies and bluebottles, urban poultry keeping and better rat or mice control. The Natural History Museum organised visits to the zoo by the Army Veterinary Corps to improve its understanding of the malarial mosquito, tsetse and plague flea.

There were fewer animal exchanges with other zoos. This was because of reduced funds for animal purchases generally. War also meant it was more dangerous to transport animals from their natural habitats. The War Office also asked the zoo not to purchase some animals – Rhesus monkeys, for example – as they were required to improve British scientists' understanding of tetanus and of gas attacks. The zoo also declined offers of pets from the public – notably parrots, now increasingly difficult to feed. The zoo had sufficient supplies for its own birds, however, having bought additional canary and millet seed early on. London Zoo suffered no direct air attack but raids made its animals restless and precautions were taken against breakages caused by air raids. For example, shutters were placed on the windows of the dangerous snakes at night.

One of the elephants at London Zoo in happier days, before the war.

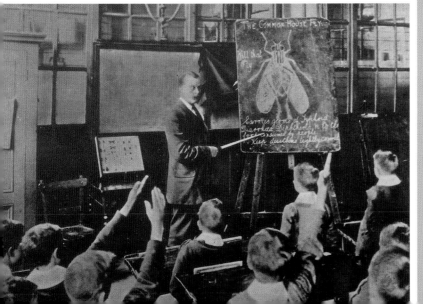

The danger of diseases spread by flies was taught to schoolchildren in Canonbury Road Council School, Islington, in 1916, published in the Illustrated London News.

21

ANIMAL WELFARE ON THE HOME FRONT

Concern for animal welfare was a well-established feature of British society in 1914, evident in legislation, the press and above all in animal charities founded since the 1820s. The Royal Society for the Prevention of Cruelty to Animals (RSPCA) was in its 90th year when war broke out. Among other charities already in existence were the National Canine Defence League (NCDL) founded in 1891, and Our Dumb Friends League (ODFL) founded in 1897. Further animal charities were to emerge during the war, notably the People's Dispensary for Sick Animals (1917). Support for animals affected by the war, both at home and overseas, was central to the work of all these organisations, and others too. Together they did much to alleviate animal suffering and prevent unnecessary deaths.

On the outbreak of the conflict, the RSPCA offered its services immediately to the War Office, primarily in terms of the care of sick and wounded horses. Although this was initially declined, in November the Society was invited to assist. It undertook training of 200 men experienced in the care of horses. They then joined the Army Veterinary Corps. The RSPCA also opened a fund to provide accommodation for horses receiving treatment overseas, and sent 180 horse ambulances, rugs, head collars and halters. The Society established 13 hospitals, caring for 13,500 horses. It also provided tented horse hospitals and

A horse wearing netting to protect it against an annoyance the Illustrated War News *described as 'the swarms of flies which have invaded the fighting area'.*

a convalescent horse depot. By March 1919 it had spent almost £200,000 to support the welfare of Army animals.

The initial purpose of ODFL was to help working animals in London. But in 1912, as a consequence of the on-going Balkan War, it set up, separately, the Blue Cross Fund to care for horses needing medical attention there. Although the League's offer of help in 1914 was rejected by the War Office (but accepted by the French), the Blue Cross Fund *was* re-established. The money raised was spent on portable forges, horse rugs and, for horses wounded in the Middle East, fly-nets.

With their menfolk away fighting, some families could no longer afford to keep their dog. The NCDL did what it could to discourage people from abandoning or having their pet put down. During the war it supplied dog biscuits and paid for 12,500 dog licences. The PDSA, founded by Maria Dickin, also aimed to help the poor by providing care for their sick and injured animals. It began in London's East End, operating from a cellar. Horse-drawn clinics soon supplemented its work.

"OUR DUMB FRIENDS' LEAGUE"
A SOCIETY FOR THE ENCOURAGEMENT OF KINDNESS TO ANIMALS.

BLUE CROSS FUND
For WOUNDED HORSES
AT THE FRONT.
DONATIONS IMMEDIATELY TO
ARTHUR J. COKE, Secretary,
58, VICTORIA STREET, LONDON, S.W.

Our Dumb Friends' League poster fundraising for the wounded horses of the war.

An original Blue Cross advertisement.

When we think of the horrors of War—when there rises before the mind the awful panorama of the battlefield—the men are not the only pathetic figures. An equal demand has been made on those noble animals who, when guided by a rider's hand, will face the cannon's mouth!

They have to fight and suffer together, but there is this difference—the horses are not free agents—they have no exhortations of patriotic duty, no visions of glory and promotion.

'DO SOMETHING' for the HORSES—
HELP THE BLUE CROSS FUND.

MASCOTS

The term 'mascot' was only popularised in the late 19th century, but what it represents is much older – in England's case, since at least the Civil War (1940s). Derived from the French for witch, a 'mascot' usually carries with it a sense of good luck and, when applied to animals, denotes a living embodiment of the group to which it belongs. There were animal mascots in all three armed services in the First World War. Individual regiments were responsible for their food and care. This was also true for ships' mascots. These were usually cats, being not only good mousers but territorial too (and thus less appropriate for the Army, which was constantly on

Just one of many extraordinary mascots at the Front (which also included owls, monkeys and goats as well as hundreds of cats and dogs): the Warwickshire Yeomanry's orangutan.

the move). Among the famous mascots of the war were Norah, Tirpitz and Poilu. When HMS *King Edward VII* was mined in 1916 there was enough time to rescue all its crew and the mascot, Norah. The subject was painted

Another extraordinary mascot: a golden eagle, reared from when he was 'nothing but a yellow ball of fluff'.

by Cyrus Cuneo and entitled 'Bulldog Rescued'.
Tirpitz, a pig, was also rescued from the German
light cruiser *Dresden*, which was sunk by HMS
Glasgow. The new ship's crew named her after
Germany's Grand Admiral and made her the
ship's mascot. She was later sold at an auction,
raising 400 guineas for the Red Cross. Her head
was subsequently mounted and presented to the
Imperial War Museum.

Poilu (a French term to mean a soldier) was a
lion, born in captivity in France. He was bought
when three months old at a Red Cross auction in
Paris for 10,000 francs. His purchaser presented
him to General Bridges of the 19th (Western)
Division to be their mascot. He was very popular,
not least when he accompanied, unleashed, the
General around the local community and into the trenches.
Bridges' successor was not so enamoured with the mascot
and arranged for Poilu to be transferred to a private animal
collection in Maidstone. His owner also acquired three other
mascots – a bear, a sheepdog and a Russian wolfhound.

The rescue of Norah the bulldog from HMS King Edward VII, *painted by Cyrus Cuneo.*

London Zoo probably acquired the most recognisable mascot.
Lieutenant Colebourn, en route to England with a Canadian
cavalry regiment, bought a bear which he named Winnipeg.
Soon abbreviated to 'Winnie', the bear was given to the zoo
when the regiment went overseas. Many enthused over him
– including one Christopher Robin, son of writer A.A. Milne.
Consequently, Milne used the name in a story he was writing,
which of course was *Winnie the Pooh*.

Colebourn on Salisbury Plain with Winnipeg as a cub, 1914.

ANIMALS AND THE RETURN OF PEACE

I n the aftermath of the Boer War (1899–1902), many sick horses left South Africa for Britain. Many died on the return, or brought diseases with them. The situation was better in 1919 but still proved controversial. Thousands of British Army horses in France were initially sold to local farmers as labour or as meat. The British public, and in particular animal charities, was furious over the latter treatment and the RSPCA threatened to withdraw its co-operation with the military. The government agreed to be more actively involved and investigate would-be purchasers' intentions.

More than 150,000 horses were sold overseas, local to where they had last served. An undignified end was not confined to France. The Middle East campaign had involved some 74,000 horses. It was impracticable or impossible to repatriate survivors. Instead, those under 12 and fit were sold to markets and farmers; the remainder was destroyed. In 1930 Major-General Brooke was appointed to the British Cavalry Brigade in Egypt. His wife, Dorothy Brooke, already an established campaigner for horse welfare,

Dorothy Brooke and one of her charges.

Dorothy Brooke and the Old War Horse committee.

accompanied him. On encountering the neglect and suffering of horses there she successfully sought funds to buy old warhorses. In 1934 she established the Old War Horse Memorial Hospital in Cairo. This evolved into an international organisation and is now known as The Brooke.

Horses underwent tests to confirm their good health before embarkation. Probably between 60,000 and 100,000 horses were returned to Britain and sold at auction. Many were bought by farmers, and others to assist with deliveries. The editor of the magazine *John Bull* suggested the horses which had served on the Front and survived should be awarded an 'Order of Merit', a badge declaring 'Treat me well – I've done my bit'.

Soldiers often befriended the dogs which they had encountered whilst serving abroad, notably in the trenches. They might wish to bring the dogs with them on their return to Britain but be unable to afford the cost – £14 per dog – of six months' quarantine. The RSPCA, Our Dumb Friends' League and the National Canine Defence League, with the Army Council's approval, agreed to cover most (£12) of this. Each owner had to pay the remaining £2. This was to ensure that the dog would be collected. The RSPCA, with the consent and co-operation of the Battersea Dogs' Home, also undertook to build 500 special kennels at the latter's quarantine site in Surrey. Dogs barred from Britain were humanely destroyed.

These injured servicemen (the man at the front having lost both hands in the conflict) are being trained in how to care for poultry. Other men learnt agricultural skills, or the care of horses or pigs.

ANIMAL HEROES

Given that they had no choice, all the animals involved in the First World War might be said to be heroes – and treated as such. Indeed, in 2014 the horse Warrior was awarded posthumously the first Honorary PDSA Dickin Medal (often dubbed the 'animals' Victoria Cross') on behalf of all animals who had served the British forces in that conflict. Those considered here are among several whose deeds made them particularly famous.

Warrior belonged to Major General Jack Seely. Both served and were inseparable throughout the war. Warrior faced entrapment in burning stables, air attacks and shelling and took part in the Battles of the Somme and Passchendaele. When peace came, Warrior returned to the Isle of Wight where he had been foaled in 1908. He died there in 1941, earning an obituary in *The Times* and the London *Evening Standard* – the latter under the banner the 'Horse the Germans could not kill'.

Jack Seely astride Warrior, his famous war horse.

Pets, dogs in particular, occasionally directly featured in the war. Jack was a stray German shepherd dog taken in and cared for by Nurse Edith Cavell in 1911. In 1914–1915 he provided cover for her as innocent middle-aged woman in German-occupied Brussels, where she assisted in helping British soldiers to escape. Jack was separated from Cavell following her arrest and after her execution, he was all but abandoned. He was eventually cared for by the Dowager Duchess of Croy, whose chateau acted as a Red Cross centre on the Franco-Belgian border. Jack died in 1923 and was eventually acquired and preserved by the Imperial War Museum.

Edith Cavell with her pet dogs, including Jack. Today, stuffed and mounted, Jack is part of the Imperial War Museum's collection.

Prince was an Irish terrier owned by Private James Brown of the First Battalion of the North Staffordshire Regiment. In September of 1914 Brown was posted to France. Mrs Brown, together with Prince, visited family in Hammersmith, London. A month after their arrival Prince went missing, and she wrote informing her husband accordingly. He replied that the dog was with him, that Prince had found him in Armentières! The RSPCA arranged for the dog's safe return home.

On the Home Front animals were mobilised to raise funds for the war effort. As a result of being auctioned almost 11,000 times and travelling 17,000 miles throughout the country, the Warboys' ('VC') Cockerel raised over £12,000 for the Red Cross.

The Warboys Cockerel.

IN REMEMBRANCE OF ANIMALS

The (involuntary) role which animals had played in the conflict and the need to remember them were not forgotten when the war ended, nor in the decades which followed.

Above and far right: the Animals in War memorial in Park Lane, London.

In November 1918 the National Canine Defence League announced that it would open a new home and hospital for stray or unwanted dogs to commemorate the work of dogs during the war. Subsequently, memorials were erected specifically to mark the contribution of horses. There are horse troughs on the Isle of Wight and in Newton, Cambridgeshire. Placed in front of the conventional village war memorial, the latter states 'to the memory of the horses who helped our armies to victory'. The front of the trough declares, 'They also served'.

Inside St Jude's church, Hampstead Garden Suburb, London, there is a memorial to horses. It was suggested by the first vicar, who had been a wartime chaplain. In 1926 Charles Lutyens, son of the church's architect Sir Edwin Lutyens, offered a bronze of his own war horse. It was stolen in the 1960s, as was its successor. The warhorse currently on display (2016) dates from 1970. The accompanying plaque is the original (1926), proclaiming the memorial to be 'in grateful and reverent memory of the Empire's horses … most obediently and often most painfully they died'. An original quotation that follows stating that 'not one of them is forgotten before God', is perhaps indicative of an increasingly mainstream and all-embracing view at the time, that animals had souls and would be reunited with their owners in heaven.

Jimmy 'the Sergeant' was a donkey born during the Battle of the Somme. Initially a regimental mascot, he was acquired by Peterborough RSPCA in 1919 and helped to raise funds for them. There is a memorial to him in Peterborough Central Park. In July 2015 a sculpture commemorating its remount depot and the horses which died in the war was unveiled in Romsey.

The Animals in War memorial was unveiled in 2004. Located at Brook Gate, Park Lane, London, it represents all animals which served, suffered and died in relation to British Imperial and Allied forces over the course of the 20th century as a whole. At its core is a large curved Portland stone wall with animals engraved in profile. They include one or more of a camel, elephant, glow worm and pigeon. A horse, mule and dog approach the wall. The inscription concludes, 'They had no choice.'

PLACES TO VISIT

Imperial War Museum
IWM London, Lambeth Road, London SE1 6HZ
IWM.org.uk

National Army Museum
Royal Hospital Road, Chelsea, London SW3 4HT
www.nam.ac.uk/research/famous-units/royal-army-veterinary-corps

Royal Army Medical Corps Museum (for the Army Veterinary Corps)
Keogh Barracks, Ash Vale, Aldershot, GU12 5RQ
www.ams-museum.org.uk

Queen's Own Hussars Museum
Lord Leycester Hospital, 60 High Street, Warwick, CV34 4BH
www.qohmuseum.org.uk

Warwickshire Yeomanry Museum
The Court House, Jury Street, Warwick CV34 4EW
www.warwickshire-yeomanry-museum.co.uk

York Army Museum
3A Tower Street, York, YO1 9SB
www.yorkshireregiment.com

Local military museums may also include a section on military use of animals (notably the horse and dog), especially museums for (former) cavalry regiments.

Imperial War Museum.